A CAULDRON OF HALLOWEEN IDEAS

Literature-Based and Cross-Curricular

by Lorrie L. Birchall

SCHOLASTIC
PROFESSIONAL BOOKS

NEW YORK • TORONTO • LONDON • AUCKLAND • SYDNEY

For Jet and J. T. Birchall

Design by Jacqueline Swensen
Cover design by Vincent Ceci
Cover illustration by Tedd Arnold
Interior illustration by Ellen Joy Sasaki

ISBN 0-590-49342-6

12 11 10 9 8 7 6 5 4 3 2   4 5 / 9

Printed in the U.S.A.

TABLE OF CONTENTS

HALLOWEEN RESEARCH SKILLS

HALLOWEEN COOKING

HALLOWEEN QUICK TRICKS AND NEAT TREATS

HALLOWEEN RESOURCES

Dear Teachers,

Halloween is an exciting time for children. A CAULDRON OF HALLOWEEN IDEAS will help you capitalize on children's fascination with Halloween to achieve many of your teaching objectives. It contains a variety of curriculum-related learning possibilities, designed to provide enjoyable and successful learning experiences. In addition, it is very "teacher-friendly." As an elementary teacher myself, I know that your time is a precious commodity.

You can use the teaching ideas and student worksheets in this book in a variety of ways—in learning centers, with pairs or cooperative groups, stapled into individual work packets, given out as bonus work or homework. Some activities are connected to thematic units on bones, monsters, and other seasonal studies, while others are more open-ended. There is a range in skill level, so that you are better able to individualize and meet the needs of your students.

Whatever your preferred teaching style, I hope that A CAULDRON OF HALLOWEEN IDEAS helps fuel your students' desire to learn, while making your challenging and very important job a little bit easier.

Happy Halloween!

Lorrie L. Birchall

Lorrie L. Birchall

HALLOWEEN-THEMED LITERATURE UNITS

Where the Wild Things Are

by Maurice Sendak

Children's Halloween literature provides an abundance of learning possibilities! It's a great starting point for developing thematic units, curricular connections, reading-writing connections, and more.

I chose *Where the Wild Things Are* as an example because it is a classic in children's literature and can be found in most children's library collections.

I hope that the following examples will provide you with new ideas for developing learning experiences for whichever Halloween books you choose.

READING SKILLS
- Pre-reading questions for children's literature, p. 9
- Vocabulary introduction, p. 10
- Sequence strips, p. 11
- Grammar out of context, p. 12

WRITING
- Write a postcard from one of the Wild Things to Max, p. 15. What would a Wild Thing want to say to Max after he returned home?
- Write a travel brochure to convince tourists to visit where the Wild Things are.
- Write a story about one of your own dreams. Did you ever dream of an adventure like Max's?

CRITICAL ANALYSIS

- What did the Wild Things think of Max?
- Why wasn't Max afraid of the Wild Things?
- How would you feel if you were Max, king of the Wild Things?
- Why did Max leave the Wild Things?
- Could Max go back to where the Wild Things are? Why or why not?

CREATIVE DRAMA

- Make puppets based on the characters in *Where the Wild Things Are*. Give a puppet show to the class.
- Role-play the part of a TV newscaster who broadcasts a special news bulletin about Max's adventure.

EXPRESSIVE ARTS

- Take a trip to where the Wild Things are! From magazines, cut out pictures of things you would bring back from your visit. Glue pictures inside the suitcase on p.17.
- Create greeting cards for the book's characters. For example, send a bon voyage card to Max for his trip to where the Wild Things are. Or send a "cheer up" card to the Wild Things, because their king went home to his supper.
- Compose music that could be played during a wild rumpus.
- Make a relief map of the place where the Wild Things live.
- Create your own Wild Thing costume from recycled materials.

RESEARCH SKILLS

- Find out more about dreams. Look up "Dreams" in encyclopedias, dictionaries, and other sources. Share your findings.
- Find out more about today's legendary "wild things" such as the Loch Ness Monster and Big Foot. Based on your research, do you believe these "wild things" exist?

SCIENCE

- Think of some real "wild things" you could find in a zoo. Decide on a way to categorize them, such as whether they are meat eaters or vegetarians; whether they have scales, fur, or skin; and whether they live on land, in the water, or in the air.

MATH

- Count all of the Wild Things.
- Max "sailed back over a year and in and out of weeks and through a day." How many hours are in one day? How many days are in one week? How many days are in one year? How many weeks are in one year?

PRE-READING QUESTIONS FOR CHILDREN'S LITERATURE

1. What is the title of the book?

2. Who is the author of the book?

3. Who is the illustrator?

4. How many pages are in the book?

5. What does the cover tell you about the book?

6. What is the copyright date of the book?
How many years ago was the book published?

7. What do you think the story is about?

8. Where do you think the story takes place?

9. Do you think this will be a realistic story or a fantasy?

10. What are you curious to find out about this story?

VOCABULARY INTRODUCTION
for *Where the Wild Things Are*

Before reading the story with your class, introduce vocabulary and stimulate your student's background knowledge (schema).

1. Synonyms: What words mean the same thing as *mischief?*

2. Antonyms: What word means the opposite of *night?*

3. Categorization: What words have something in common with the category "Wild Things?"

4. Homonyms: What are other ways to spell…

      eye? (I)

      night? (knight)

Does the other spelling mean the same thing?

5. Context: According to the context of the story, what words make sense in the blanks?

"…and into the night of his very _____ room where he _____ his supper waiting for _____ and it was _____ hot."

6. Dictionary usage: In your dictionary, find the word *wild*. What is the definition?

7. Parts of speech: Which words show action?
      a. gnashed
      b. eyes
      c. roared
      d. terrible

8. Structural analysis: Which words have the same "a" sound as in Max?
      a. day
      b. gnashed
      c. claws
      d. back

SEQUENCE STRIPS
for *Where the Wild Things Are*

DIRECTIONS:

1. Read *Where the Wild Things Are* by Maurice Sendak.

2. Cut out the sequence strips below.

3. Put the sequence strips in the correct order and then glue them on a blank piece of paper.

4. Put your name on your paper.

Max sailed home.

A forest grew in Max's room.

Max was sent to bed without eating.

The wild rumpus began.

Max became king of the Wild Things.

Max found his supper waiting for him.

Max sailed off in a boat to where the Wild Things are.

GRAMMAR OUT OF CONTEXT MAX'S MAD LIB

When adjectives, nouns, and verbs are indiscriminately placed in a passage out of context, students find the result very humorous. They come to realize that word choice is very important and that context clues help to convey meaning.

DIRECTIONS:

1. Review *nouns* (people, places, and things),
adjectives (describing words),
verbs (action words),
and brainstorm many examples of each.

2. Give each cooperative group a copy of Max's Mad Lib (p. 13–14). Have students write words requested in each blank in Section A. For example:

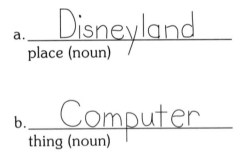

a. Disneyland
place (noun)

b. Computer
thing (noun)

3. Read the passage in section B to the class, leaving the blanks. Ask groups to *verbally* insert the corresponding nouns, verbs, and adjectives from section A into the passage. It probably sounds pretty silly! Have groups read their filled-in passages aloud.

3. Using the context of the passage, have groups brainstorm words that would make sense in Max's Mad Lib and write them in section B.

5. Discuss the importance of using context to understand the meaning of a passage.

MAX'S MAD LIB

DIRECTIONS: Fill in each blank in Section A then transfer each word onto Section B.

SECTION A

_____
1. place (noun)

_____
2. thing (noun)

_____
3. thing (noun)

_____
4. description (adjective)

_____
5. things (nouns)

_____
6. action (verb) — present tense

_____
7. action (verb) — present tense

_____
8. action (verb) — present tense

_____
9. thing (noun)

_____
10. thing (noun)

_____
11. description (adjective)

SECTION B

Max had a dream that he went to visit _____ .
1. place (noun)

He brought _____ along with him. Unfortunately,
2. thing (noun)

he forgot to bring his _____ .
3. thing (noun)

When he finally arrived at his destination, he found

_____Wild Things waiting for him.
    4. description (adjective)

They made him king of the _____ .
                                 5. things (nouns)

     The Wild Things liked to _____ and
                                   6. action (verb)

_____ all the time.
    7. action (verb)

Max got very tired of it, so he decided to _____
                                      8. action (verb)

home. He woke up in his _____
                 9. thing (noun)

and found his _____ waiting for him. It was still
          10. thing (noun)

_____ .
    11. description (adjective)

WILD POSTCARDS

DIRECTIONS:

1. After reading *Where the Wild Things Are,* have students write a postcard from one of the Wild Things to Max. What would a Wild Thing want to say to Max after he returned home?

2. To make postcards, photocopy the example below and glue it onto oak tag.

3. Share examples of postcards, then show students how to write and address them.

4. Have students illustrate a scene from the book on the back.

TO: _____

TAKE A TRIP TO WHERE THE WILD THINGS ARE

MATERIALS:

magazines or catalogs
glue
scissors
crayons
construction paper

DIRECTIONS:

1. Ask children to cut double suitcases from large sheets of construction paper or oak tag, following the pattern on the next page.

2. From magazines and catalogs, allow students to cut out pictures of things they would bring back from their trip.

3. Have the students glue the pictures inside their suitcases.

4. Allow students to share their "souvenirs" with the class.

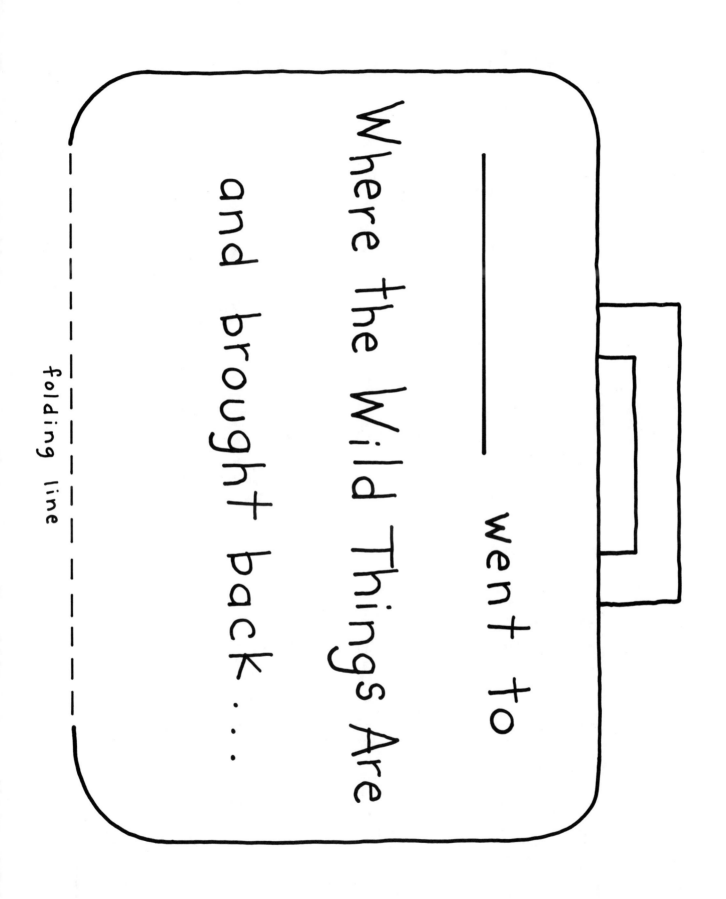

_____ went to Where the Wild Things Are and brought back . . .

The Vanishing Pumpkin

by Tony Johnston
pictures by Tommy dePaola

SUMMARY: A 700-year-old woman and an 800-year-old man go searching for their stolen pumpkin.

WRITING

● Write cinquain poems for each character and share them with the class.

Format:

1 noun
2 adjectives
3 verbs or participles
4 adjectives or 1 statement
1 noun (synonym for top noun)

Example:

woman
old, hungry
flying, muttering, tricking
likes pumpkin pie
witch

RESEARCH SKILLS

● Find out the ages of the longest living man and woman in the *Guinness Book of World Records*.

READING SKILLS

● Compare traits of each character to determine similarities and differences.

	magic powers	old	hungry	short
700-year-old woman	X	X	X	
800-year-old man	X	X	X	
ghoul			X	X
rapscallion			X	X
varmint			X	X
900-year-old wizard	X	X	X	

MATH

- What is the sum of their ages?

  The old woman was 700 years old.

  The old man was 800 years old.

  The old wizard was 900 years old.

- In what year was each born?

CRITICAL THINKING

The round orange sun reminded the 700-year-old woman of a pumpkin.

Think of things that are round.

Think of things that are orange.

Think of things that are both round and orange.

Example:

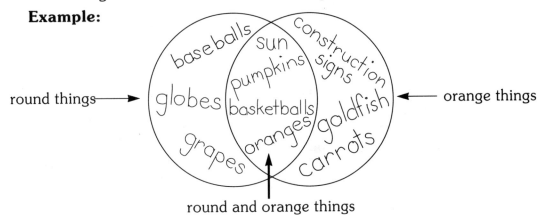

round things →

← orange things

round and orange things

ART

- Make a collage.

Cut a sponge into a pumpkin shape. Dip the sponge into thinned orange tempera paint. Stamp the pumpkin sponge several times on white or black construction paper for a collage effect. Display around the classroom for a Halloween atmosphere.

COOKING

- Make a pumpkin pie.

Ingredients:

3 eggs
pastry shell
16-oz. can of pumpkin
1/2 cup milk
5-oz. can evap. milk

3/4 cup sugar
1/2 tsp. ginger
1/2 tsp. nutmeg
1 1/2 tsp. cinnamon

Directions:

1. In a mixing bowl, add spices to pumpkin mix.

2. Add eggs and milks.

3. Pour pumpkin mixture into a pastry shell.

4. Bake at 375° for 50-55 min. Cool. Serve and enjoy!

Harriet's Halloween Candy

by Nancy Carlson

SUMMARY: Harriet discovers that sharing her Halloween candy with her little brother makes her feel better than eating it all herself.

WRITING

- Write about one of your own Halloween trick or treat experiences.
- Write an advertisement for a new Halloween candy that is delicious, yet nutritious. Design a poster to accompany it.

RESEARCH SKILLS

- Research the origin of sugar. What does sugar do to your body? Why is it important to brush our teeth after eating candy?

CRITICAL THINKING

- How could Harriet have avoided getting sick from eating too much candy? (e.g., rationing)
- When is it hard to share?
- Why is sharing important?
- Why did Harriet feel guilty when she said that the candy was hers alone?
- How do you think Walt felt when Harriet shared her candy?

SCIENCE/ HEALTH

- Discuss the four food groups. Why is candy not considered one of the food groups?
- Discuss the importance of having an adult check all Halloween candy before it is eaten.

MATH

- Make a bar graph of the Halloween candy you collected.

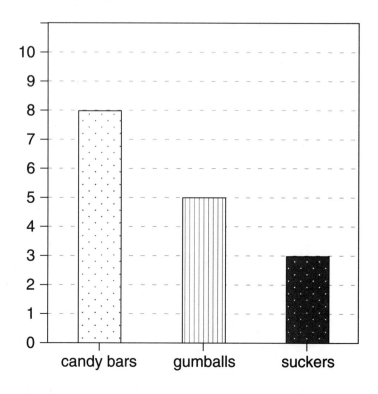

HALLOWEEN LANGUAGE ARTS

POETRY

POETRY IN A LEARNING CENTER

Poetry Sequence Strips: Write a familiar poem on tag board. Cut the lines into strips students put in correct sequence. Keep the strips in a plastic bag labeled with the poem's title. Store "poem bags" in a shoebox. You can also hang bags from a witch's broomstick or display them on a bulletin board as part of a Halloween theme.

Poetry Recordings: Students take turns reading poems into a tape recorder. After children hear themselves read, they can reread the poem to practice their expression, fluency, intonation, and so on.

Variation: Create a class poetry tape for the Listening Center. Every student practices a favorite Halloween poem, then reads it on the tape— starting where the previous student left off. Try to recruit some "mystery readers" such as the school principal, librarian, or janitor.

Class Collection: Students write out favorite Halloween poems and illustrate them for a class anthology of Halloween poetry.

Read-a-Poem: Write one poem per index card and keep a file box stocked full in a Reading Center.

POETRY AS DRAMA

Encourage students to act out poems and be dramatic! Have the class make props and costumes to accompany the reading. Hold a performance for parents and/or other classes.

THE CLOZE PROCEDURE WITH POETRY

Write out a Halloween poem, leaving a few blank spaces. Ask students to think of words that would make sense in the blanks. Compare student responses with the author's completed poem.

Three Ghostesses

Three little ghostesses,
(*Sitting*) on postesses,
Eating buttered (*toastesses*),
Greasing their wristesses,
Oh, what beastesses
To make such (*feastesses*)!
—Anonymous

POETRY CHORAL READING

Write Halloween poems on large sheets of butcher paper and use clothespins to string them around the classroom. Take every opportunity to recite the poems as a class.

POETRY AS A WRITING STIMULUS

Poetry provides models of many different writing styles and offers various examples of descriptive and figurative language. Read many kinds of poems to encourage students to write their own poetry.

POETRY "TAG"

One student poet stands to recite a poem and then "tags" another poet (teachers included!) to recite the next poem. Poets can memorize their poems or read from the poetry selection hanging around the room.

Name _____

RHYME TIME

DIRECTIONS: With a partner, brainstorm as many *rhyming* words as you can for these Halloween words.

ghost

_____

_____

_____

_____

_____

scary

_____

_____

_____

_____

_____

bat

_____

_____

_____

_____

_____

★ **BONUS:** Write a poem together, using your rhyming words.

JOKES

JOKES IN A LEARNING CENTER

Reading Center: Write each joke separately on one side of a 3x5 card with the punch line written on the back. Store jokes in a labeled file box or manila envelope.

Listening Center: Tape-record jokes from a Halloween joke book. Place the book as well as the tape in the Listening Center. Students read along as they listen to the tape.

Writing Center: Make shape booklets from lined-white writing paper stapled to the Herbert Monster cover sheet (see page 25). Students write their favorite jokes in the shape booklets. They may also want to include their own Halloween jokes, or a few from page 26.

JOKES IN A READING SKILLS LESSON

Many jokes contain excellent examples of homonyms and plays on words.

Examples: What do you do if you meet a blue monster?
(Cheer him up.)

Monster Motel is next to which lake?
(Lake Erie.)

What would you call a monster who ate his mother's sister?
(An aunt-eater.)

JOKES FOR PAIRED READING

Because jokes are meant to be shared, joke books are highly-motivating reading for many students.

JOKES AS DRAMA

Invite students to memorize a few of their favorite Halloween jokes and have a stand-up comedy hour! They might like to begin with A Sampling of Herbert Monster's Jokes on page 26.

MONSTER PATTERN FOR SHAPE BOOKLET

HERBERT ♥ HALLOWEEN JOKES

A SAMPLING OF HERBERT MONSTER'S JOKES

You might like to include some of these jokes in your shape booklet.

How does Herbert Monster count to 21?
   (*On his fingers.*)

Why wasn't Herbert's best friend sorry that he lost his head?
   (*He still had the other one.*)

What did Herbert say
to his "goulfriend" Marsha
at the Halloween dance?
   (*I want to hold your hand,*
   hand, hand, hand, hand, etc.)

What is Herbert's favorite TV show?
   (*Monsterpiece Theater.*)

What did Herbert Monster eat after
   the dentist pulled his tooth?
   (*The dentist.*)

Why was Herbert Monster afraid to
   leave his haunted house?
   (*He didn't like what he read in his horror-scope.*)

What city is Herbert from?
   (*Monstrosity.*)

What is Herbert's favorite game?
   (*Hide and shriek.*)

VOCABULARY

bat	troll	goblin	monster
mummy	pumpkin	scary	ghost
witch	haunt	skeleton	owl
October	spooky	Halloween	vampire
Dracula	Frankenstein	Autumn	jack-o'-lantern

Try these Halloween vocabulary activities in cooperative groupings and learning centers.

HALLOWEEN DOMINOES (2-4 players)

To make dominoes, draw a line down the center of 20 3x5 cards. On each side write a Halloween vocabulary word from the list above. Make sure every Halloween vocabulary word is written twice, but on different cards. Store in a plastic bag. (Optional: Laminate for durability.)

Follow the rules for regular dominoes, and have students read the words aloud as they put their dominoes down for a match.

Provide additional 3x5 cards so students can create their own Halloween vocabulary dominoes.

ALPHABETIZE HALLOWEEN VOCABULARY WORDS

Write each Halloween vocabulary word on a 3x5 card. Working in pairs or groups, have students put the Halloween words in alphabetical order.

Challenge students to make up sentences that include two, three, four, or more Halloween vocabulary words.

Extension: Read Halloween A B C by Eve Merriam
(Macmillan Publishing, 1987.)

VOCABULARY (continued)

SOMETHING IN COMMON

List the Halloween vocabulary words on a chart. Have students work in small groups to pair up all 20 words. Each pair must have *something* in common. Share all the ideas.

Examples:
bat & owl: both fly, both are 3-letter words
Dracula & Frankenstein: both are famous movie monsters
skeleton & spooky: both begin with "s"

SEMANTIC MAPPING

Give each small group one Halloween vocabulary word to map. Have students brainstorm related words and "map" all the connections on a blank sheet of paper. Students should then try to suggest labels to organize the relationship. Share the maps and display them. This is also a great pre-writing activity.

Jack-o-lantern

carving   candles

TV Show:

The Great
Pumpkin
Charlie Brown

Fall Season

October

leaves
falling   cool
weather

Pumpkin

Appearance

orange   sphere
              shape

large

Food

bread   seed

pie

CREATIVE PERFORMANCES

Give each small group three Halloween vocabulary words and ask each to devise a short poem, song, or TV commercial using them. Set a time limit for the groups to work on their creative performances, and then invite them to perform for the class.

DEFINITIONS

DIRECTIONS:

1. Write a Halloween vocabulary word on the chalkboard, for example: **monster.**

2. Discuss dictionary definitions—how words are located alphabetically, what information is/is not included, etc.

3. Read some dictionary definitions as examples and discuss their format.

4. Have small groups write a dictionary style definition for the Halloween vocabulary word without consulting a dictionary. Students should rely on their previous experience to write a definition.

You may also provide each group with a different Halloween vocabulary word to define.

5. Have group spokespeople read aloud the group definitions.

6. Ask groups to look up the dictionary definition and compare it to the students' definition. What are the similarities? Differences? Are there different meanings for the same word?

EXTENSIONS:

1. Discuss multiple meanings (homonyms), using the word monster as an example.

"A fabulous being compounded of elements from various human and animal forms."

"An animal or plant having structural defects or deformities."

"Any very large animal, plant or object."

"One who inspires horror or disgust."

> — The American Heritage Dictionary of the English Language, (Houghton Mifflin Co., 1981).

2. Have groups illustrate each meaning of the word.

3. As a class or in groups, brainstorm examples and non-examples of the word.

monster:

Examples	Non-Examples
King Kong	Thumbelina
Mummy	Little Red Riding Hood
Big Foot	Mickey Mouse

A CLASS DICTIONARY

MATERIALS:

white drawing paper
crayons
pencils
pens
dictionaries (for reference)

Glopmonster. A three-legged monster who likes to eat gloppy oatmeal at midnight.

DIRECTIONS:

1. Brainstorm possibilities for unique imaginary Halloween creatures. Focus on specific, eccentric characteristics as you write creative definitions for the creatures.

2. Review dictionary use; how words are located in alphabetical order, definitions, etc.

3. Assign each student a letter, or have students work in pairs or groups to create an imaginary Halloween creature beginning with the letter assigned and write its description.

4. Students then illustrate their creatures. (Note: For some students, it may be easier to illustrate the creature first, and then write its description.)

5. Bind all of the definitions into a class Halloween dictionary and display.

HALLOWEEN WRITING

FREAKY FAIRY TALES

You and your students can probably recognize several Halloween characters in familiar fairy tales. For instance…

"Jack and the Beanstalk" (giant)

"Three Billy Goats Gruff" (troll)

"Beauty and the Beast" (beast)

"Rapunzel" (witch)

"Hansel and Gretal" (witch)

As a class, rewrite (or retell) well-known fairy tales as Halloween monster tales. For example: "The Three Bears" might become "The Three Monsters."

Other possibilities include: "The Gingerbread Monster," "The Town Monster and the Country Monster," "Snow White and the Seven Monsters," and "Little Red Riding Monster."

SCARY STARTERS

WRITING ACTIVITY IDEAS

- For further inspiration, read aloud *The Mysteries of Harris Burdick* by Chris Van Allsburg (Houghton Mifflin, 1984). The book contains a series of very eerie black and white illustrations with captions.

- As an alternative, have groups use Scary Starters to begin an oral tale. After groups practice their story, they can present them to the class.

- Give each small group of three to four students one Scary Starter with which to begin a short story. Have groups share their stories, and then compile them into a class book. Or staple a pumpkin cover (page 33) to each booklet.

1. It was a cold Halloween night when I saw the. . .

2. The mad scientist was creating a new monster that could. . .

3. The large cauldron of purple liquid started to boil when. . .

4. I got an eerie feeling when I heard. . .

5. The mysterious object started floating in the air and. . .

6. The Halloween pumpkin turned into a. . .

7. The black cat started to crouch and hiss when. . .

8. Something in the closet was making a strange noise, so I opened the door and. . .

9. I couldn't believe my eyes when I saw. . .

10. As I carefully entered the haunted house, the door shut behind me and. . .

11. Make up your own Scary Starter.

PUMPKIN PATTERN FOR WRITING BOOKLETS

staple

DIRECTIONS:

1. Cut out a pumpkin shape from orange construction paper.

2. Staple lined writing paper to the pumpkin shape. Cut the lined pages to pumpkin form.

3. Keep the pumpkin-shaped booklets in the Writing Center.

Name _____

SHRIEK SPEAK

DIRECTIONS: With a partner, write the *dialogue* for these Halloween characters. If you like, role-play the characters for the class.

HALLOWEEN MATH

JOURNEY THROUGH THE PUMPKIN PATCH

(Subtraction board game)

PREPARATIONS:

1. Photocopy the game board on page 36 and the student directions below.

2. If desired, color the game board for added appeal.

3. Glue the game board and student directions to a file folder and place in the Math Center. (Optional: Laminate for durablilty.)

4. Assemble other materials: two number cubes and markers for players.

DIRECTIONS: (2-4 players)

1. Roll two number cubes.

2. Subtract the smaller number from the larger number.

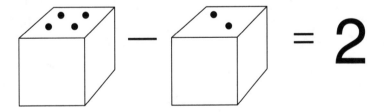

3. Move your marker that many spaces.

4. The game is over when all the players have made it to the giant jack-o'-lantern.

Variation: Roll the number cubes. Add the numbers together and move your marker that many spaces.

JOURNEY THROUGH THE PUMPKIN PATCH

START

GO AHEAD 2

GO BACK TO START

MOVE BACK 1

MOVE AHEAD 3

ROLL AN EXTRA TURN

ROLL AN EXTRA TURN

GO BACK 2

MOVE AHEAD 1

MOVE AHEAD 3

MOVE BACK 1

ROLL AN EXTRA TURN

MOVE AHEAD 1

MOVE BACK 2

HOW BIG IS YOUR PUMPKIN?

MATERIALS:

one pumpkin for each small group

scales (bathroom scales work great)

measuring tapes (or wrap a string around the pumpkin's circumference and measure it on a ruler or yardstick)

rulers, yardsticks

DIRECTIONS:

1. Introduce and discuss the meanings of these measurement terms:

estimate	inches (in.) / centimeters (cm.)
measure	pounds (lb.) / kilograms (kg.)
weight	most / least
circumference	largest / smallest
difference	

2. Have students work in small groups to weigh and measure the pumpkins. Give each group one worksheet and ask all participants to include their names.

Name _____

HOW BIG IS YOUR PUMPKIN?

PUMPKIN WEIGHT

1. Before weighing: *Estimate* how much you think

the pumpkin weighs. I think the pumpkin weighs

_____ pounds (lb.)/kilograms (kg.).

2. Now weigh the pumpkin. How much does the pumpkin actually weigh?

_____ lb./kg.

3. What is the *difference* between your *estimate* and the pumpkin's actual

weight? (Hint: Use subtraction.) _____ lb./kg.

PUMPKIN CIRCUMFERENCE

1. Before measuring: *Estimate* the *circumference* of the pumpkin. I think

the circumference of the pumpkin is

_____ inches (in.)/centimeters (cm.).

2. Now measure the pumpkin. What is the actual circumference of the

pumpkin? _____ in./cm.

3. What is the *difference* between your *estimate* and the pumpkin's actual

circumference? _____ in./cm.

Name _____

HOW BIG IS YOUR PUMPKIN?

CLASS COMPARISON OF PUMPKINS

1. The pumpkin that weighed the **most** was _____ pounds (lb.)/

kilograms (kg.).

2. The pumpkin that weighed the **least** was _____ lb./kg.

3. What was the **difference** in weight between them? _____ lb./kg.

4. The pumpkin that had the **largest** circumference was

_____ inches (in.)/centimeters (cm.).

5. The pumpkin the had the **smallest** circumference was

_____ in./cm.

6. What was the **difference** between the largest and smallest

circumference? _____ in./cm.

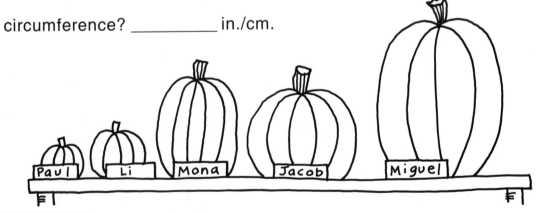

EXTENSION

What things weigh about the same as your pumpkin?

1. _____

2. _____

3. _____

Name _____

MEASURING MUMMIES

DIRECTIONS TO TEACHER:

1. Introduce and discuss these words and their meanings:

measure   inches (in.) / centimeter (cm.)

width   feet (ft.) / meter (m.)

length

2. Divide the class into groups of three or four students. Give each group a long sheet of butcher paper, a marker, and a copy of the worksheet below.

3. Each group traces around one student on the sheet of butcher paper.

4. The group then measures various parts of the "mummy" and records the measurements on the worksheet.

5. Have groups color the mummies, then cut them out for display.

---

1. Measure the mummy from the top of the head to the bottom of the feet.

_____feet (ft.)/meter (m.) _____inches (in.)/centimeters (cm.)

2. Measure the *length* of the legs.

left leg _____ ft./m. _____ in./cm.

right leg _____ ft./m. _____ in./cm.

3. Measure the *length* of the arms.

left arm _____ ft./m. _____ in./cm.

right arm _____ ft./m. _____ in./cm.

4. Measure the *width* of the head. How long is it across from ear to ear?

_____ in./cm.

40

GRAPHING GHOULS

Copy the chart below on the board or use an overhead projector.
Ask students which Halloween character is their favorite. Place an X next
to that character.

mummy	
ghost	
troll	
skeleton	
witch	
goblin	
vampire	

Which Halloween character is most popular? _____

Which Halloween character is least popular? _____

Name _____

CALENDAR CHALLENGE

DIRECTIONS: Fill in the dates on the calendar on page 43. Then use the calendar to find the answers to the first eight questions.

1. How many Tuesdays are in the month of October? _____

2. What day of the week is October 14th? _____

3. Halloween is on October 31st. Mark it on your calendar. What day of

the week is Halloween? _____

4. What is the date of the second Thursday of October? _____

5. October 27th is on what day of the week? _____

6. How many days are in one week? _____

7. How many days are in the month of October? _____

8. How many Saturdays are there in October? _____

BONUS:

★ October is in what season? _____

★ Columbus Day is celebrated on what day? _____

★ Who in the class has a birthday in October?

_____

_____

_____

Name _____

CALENDAR CHALLENGE
October 199___

SUNDAY	MONDAY	TUESDAY	WEDNESDAY	THURSDAY	FRIDAY	SATURDAY

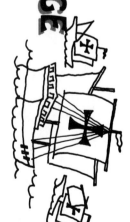

SPIDER WEB COORDINATES

MATERIALS:

graph paper
pencil
ruler

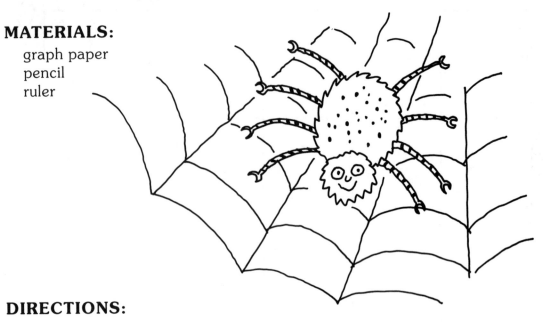

DIRECTIONS:

1. For a class activity, use an overhead projector. On graph paper, label the y-axis A–E. Label the x-axis 1–5.

2. Connect the following coordinates to create a spider web pattern: (E,1) (D,2) (C,3) (B,4) (A,5).

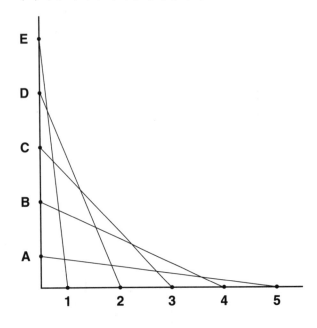

3. Let pairs of students experiment with various coordinates to create differently shaped "webs."

★ Bonus: What is the pattern to the coordinates?

Name _____

FRIGHTENING FRACTIONS

A **fraction** is a part of a whole or group. For example, "Color 2/3 of the squares" is another way to think of "Color 2 out of 3 squares."

1. Color 4/5 (4 out of five) of the cats black.

2. Color 2/3 (2 out of 3) of the jack-o'-lanterns orange.

3. Color 1/2 (1 out of 2 parts) of the witch's hat purple.

4. Color 6/8 (6 out of 8) of the spiders red.

5. Color 1/4 (1 out of 4) of the ghosts green.

6. Write your own Frightening Fraction problem for your partner.

_____

Name _____

PUZZLING PATTERNS

DIRECTIONS: Look at the pattern in each row. Draw what comes next.

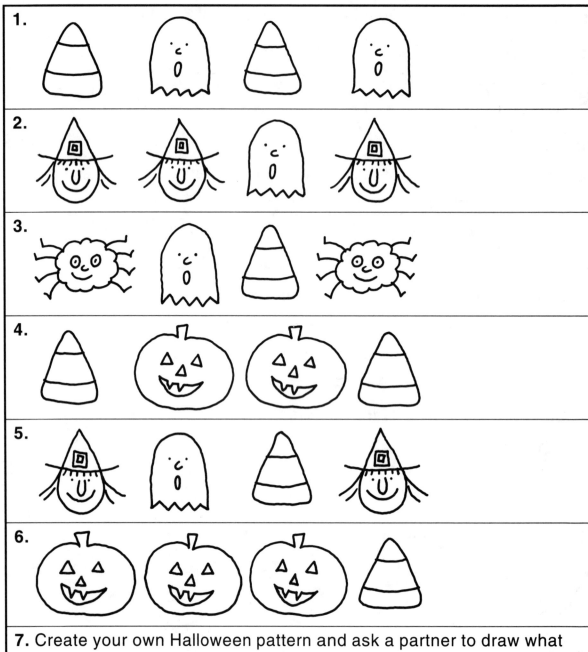

7. Create your own Halloween pattern and ask a partner to draw what comes next.

HALLOWEEN MUSIC AND ART

MONSTERLY MELODIES AND BEASTLY BEATS

IN A READING LESSON

Before singing a Halloween song, use an overhead projector to show the lyrics on a blank wall. As a class, read the words to the song together. Explain any unknown words. As an extension, have students underline rhyming words.

You may want to use words from a favorite Halloween song for vocabulary enrichment.

AS A WRITING STIMULUS

Have students change well-known nursery rhymes or holiday songs into Halloween songs. For examples, see *Marvin's Favorite Halloween Songs* by Tom Armstrong (Centerstrom Publishing, 1985).

Have students write scary tales while listening to recorded Halloween songs.

AS AN INSPIRATION FOR ART

Have students create a drawing, painting, or collage inspired by a Halloween song.

Using recycled materials, students can make and decorate instruments to use while singing Halloween songs.

FOR LISTENING AND RHYTHM SKILLS

As a class, clap the beats of a Halloween song with, and then without, the accompanying music. Have students listen for repeat patterns.

Play and compare two pieces of Halloween music. Discuss the mood each creates and how it does so. (Tempo, use of "flat" keys, and so forth.)

WITH MOVEMENT

Have students create appropriate hand and body movements to accompany a Halloween song.

CREEPY CRAYON RESIST

MATERIALS:

white drawing paper
crayons
newspapers
black tempera paint
wide paintbrush

DIRECTIONS:

1. Have students draw a Halloween scene with a thick layer of crayon on white drawing paper.

2. After placing the picture on newspaper, students brush one coat of black tempera paint over the entire picture. The crayoned areas will resist the paint.

3. Let dry and display.

BOTTLED MONSTERS

MATERIALS:

oak tag
scissors
white construction paper
crayons, pens, markers

DIRECTIONS:

1. Make various bottle-shaped templates from oak tag. See page 49 for an example.

2. Students trace the bottle shape on white construction paper, then draw the monsters inside.

3. Encourage students to fill the bottles as completely as possible.

4. Stack bottles to display, or arrange them along a chalkboard ledge.

PATTERN FOR BOTTLED MONSTERS

DESIGN A COSTUME

- Have students brainstorm various kinds of unique Halloween costumes. List them on a chart or chalkboard.
- Introduce the paper doll shape (see page 51) and show the examples of the paper doll in various costumes. If possible, enlarge the examples or use an overhead projector.
- Discuss and show students how to design costumes for the doll.

MATERIALS:

oak tag   glue
construction paper   markers
scissors   crayons

DIRECTIONS:

1. Cut out the doll. (Photocopy paper will work, but oak tag provides greater strength.)

2. Lay the doll down on construstion paper.

3. Draw an outline of the doll's costume, slightly larger than the doll.

4. Cut out the costume and glue it onto the paper doll.

5. Using markers or crayons, add details (hair, eyes, mouth, belt buckles, buttons, etc.).

6. Give your doll a name. Of course, your doll can be a girl or boy!

- Display all the costumed paper dolls on a bulletin board. Add a label with the names of the doll and the costume designer.

DESIGN A COSTUME

BEWITCHING APPLES

Turn ripe autumn apples into wrinkled old witches!

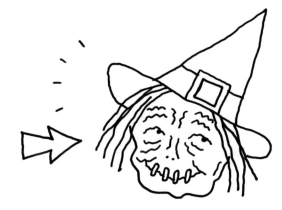

MATERIALS:

FOR APPLE HEADS
one apple per student
peelers
small paring knives
cotton balls
lemon juice
salt
shellac (spray)

FOR DECORATING
glue
scissors
colored pins or cloves for eyes
rice for teeth
cotton balls and colored yarn for hair
construction paper cones for hats

DIRECTIONS:

1. With adult help and supervision, students peel and core apples, then stuff the core with cotton balls.

2. Using a small paring knife, students gently carve the facial features—eye sockets, nose, and mouth. Advise them not to carve too deeply, because the lines will deepen as the apples dry.

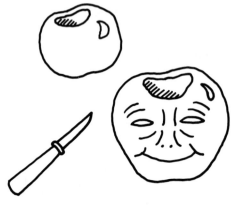

3. Have students dip the apples in lemon juice, then cover them with salt. This step helps prevent the apples from shrinking too much.

4. Place apples in a 100° oven for five hours. Then let them dry at room temperature for one week.

5. Wash and dry the apples, then spray them with shellac.

6. Add eyes, teeth, hair, and hats.

NOTE: Be sure children have adequate adult help and supervision.

Other suggested idea: Have students create witches' heads from self-hardening clay or paper-mâché. Decorate as instructed above.

HALLOWEEN PUZZLES AND GAMES

MONSTER TONGUE TWISTERS

DIRECTIONS:

1. Choose a letter to use as an example for writing an alliteration.

2. As a class, brainstorm words that begin with that letter. Using the sheet on page 54, list the words under the appropriate column: Describing Words (adjectives), Naming Words (nouns), or Action Words (verbs).

3. Together, choose words from the lists to write an alliteration, or tongue twister.

Letter "G"

DESCRIBING WORDS	NAMING WORDS	ACTION WORDS
gooey	garden	glops
green	grass	grew
grumpy	grasshopper	grumbles
giant	Gordon	gallop
	grapes	

ALLITERATION:

Gordon, the grumpy green monster, grew giant grapes in the garden.

4. After partners or small groups write their own monster alliterations, have students share the resulting tongue twisters.

53

Name _____

MONSTER TONGUE TWISTERS

With a partner or a small group, choose a letter of the alphabet. Then brainstorm words that begin with that letter. Write them in the appropriate columns. Finally, choose words from the lists to write a monster tongue twister that you can share with the class.

Letter _____

DESCRIBING WORDS	NAMING WORDS	ACTION WORDS

MONSTER TONGUE TWISTER

_____

_____

_____

Name _____

What does Halloween make *you* think of? Write your ideas below or brainstorm first with a group or a partner.

HALLOWEEN makes me think of...

MIND WINDERS

In small groups, brainstorm answers to the following questions. What are the funniest answers? The scariest?

1. What things do monsters like to eat that are yellow?

2. What would Dracula do with an old toothbrush?

3. How many ways could you compliment a monster?

4. What things could a witch ride other than a broom?

5. What are some good professions for a ghost?

6. What are some uses for a pumpkin?

7. What sports would Frankenstein play?

8. What are Dracula's favorite books?

9. What vacation spots would a mummy like to visit?

10. What games would a ghost enjoy?

CREEPY COMPARISONS

DIRECTIONS: With a partner, look at the two italicized words in the first line. How are they related? Compare the second line in the same way and fill in the missing word.

1. *Wings* are to *bats*

as _____ are to *fish*.

2. *Orange* is to *pumpkin*

as _____ is to *tomato*.

3. *Casper* is to *ghost*

as *Dracula* is to _____.

4. *Halloween* is to *October*

as *Thanksgiving* is to _____.

5. *Sweater is to Autumn*

as *bathing suit* is to _____.

6. *Jack-o'-lantern is to Halloween*

as *Cupid* is to _____.

7. *Bats* are to *caves*

as _____ are to *haunted houses*.

8. *Pumpkin* is to *vegetable*

as *apple* is to _____.

9. *Brooms* are to *witches*

as _____ are to *people*.

10. *Fangs* are to *vampires*

as _____ are to *people*.

FOLLOW BIG FOOT ACROSS THE ALPHABET

DIRECTIONS:

1. Make 26 left and right Big Feet using oak tag or colored construction paper. You can blow up the pattern on page 59 for *really* big feet.

2. Label each pair of feet with a capital and a lower-case letter for *every* letter of the alphabet. (If possible, laminate for durability.)

ACTIVITIES:

ALPHA-BODY LINE UP: A cooperative class effort! Every student receives a pair of letter feet given out at random. Students "skate" on their feet to line up in correct alphabetical sequence.

BIG FOOT CENTER ACTIVITY: Three to five students can work together to match lower-case and capital letters, then put the pairs into ABC order.

BIG FOOT PATHWAYS: Tape letters on the floor in ABC order around the classroom. Students follow the pathway to a monster trivia question, a center activity, Halloween books, or other goal. Students can also attach footprints to stomp across bulletin boards and classroom walls!

BIG FOOT PATTERN

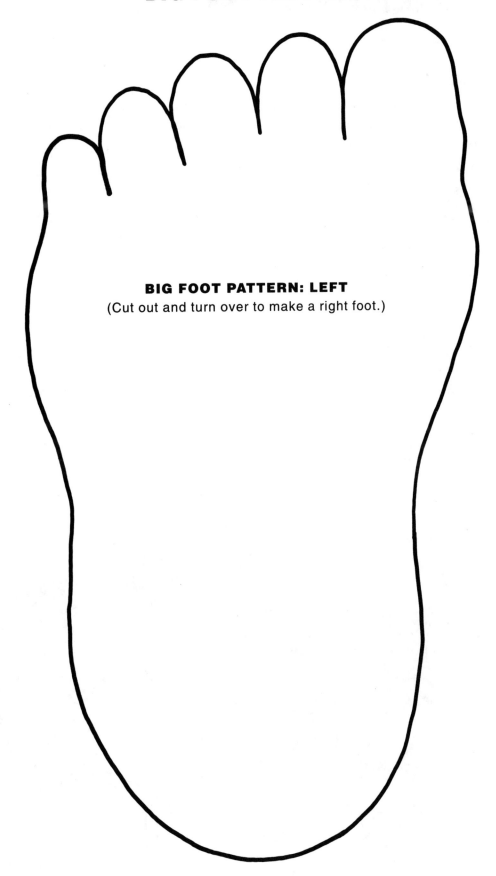

BIG FOOT PATTERN: LEFT
(Cut out and turn over to make a right foot.)

CONCENTRATION

(Memory game)

PREPARATION:

1. Make two copies of each page of Halloween Concentration cards (pages 61 and 62). Color the characters with markers for added appeal.

2. Cut apart the cards. There should be **two** of each Halloween character.

3. Glue each character to a 3x5 card. Make sure all the 3x5 cards are the same color. (Optional: Laminate the cards for durability.)

4. Place all the Halloween Concentration cards and the student directions below in a large plastic bag. The Halloween Concentration game is ready for a learning center, game area, or activity table.

GAME INSTRUCTIONS:

1. Lay all the cards *face down* so that you cannot see the Halloween characters.

2. Each player gets a chance to turn over any two cards, trying to get a match.

3. If the player gets a match, then he or she gets another chance. If not, the next player tries to get a match.

4. The game is over when players have picked up all the cards.

5. The player with the most pairs wins the game!

CONCENTRATION CARDS

Gordon Ghost

Milton Monster

Boris Bat

Wendy Witch

Frank N. Stein

Jack O. Lantern

Tommy Troll

Sammy Scarecrow

CONCENTRATION CARDS

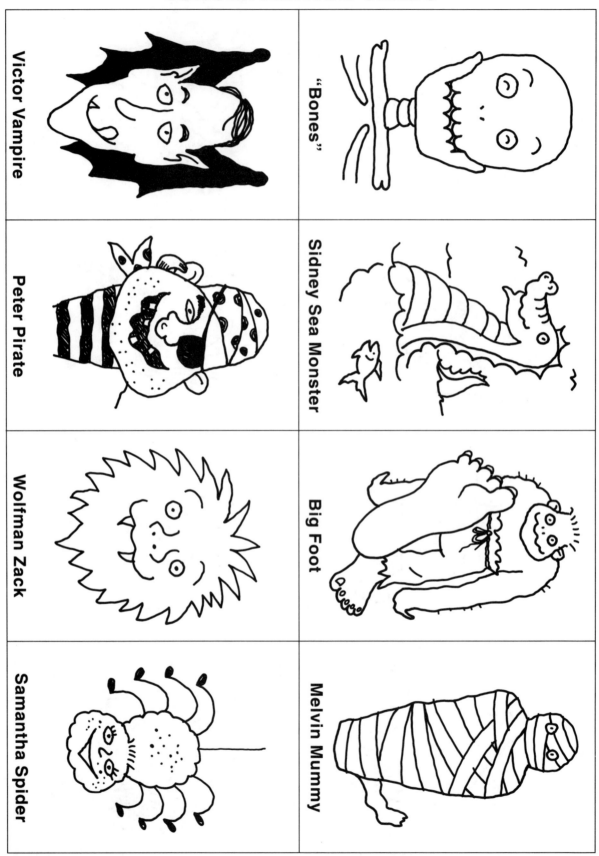

Victor Vampire

"Bones"

Peter Pirate

Sidney Sea Monster

Wolfman Zack

Big Foot

Samantha Spider

Melvin Mummy

62

Name _____

BE A DETECTIVE

DIRECTIONS: One Halloween item in each row is *not* like the others.
Draw what is missing.

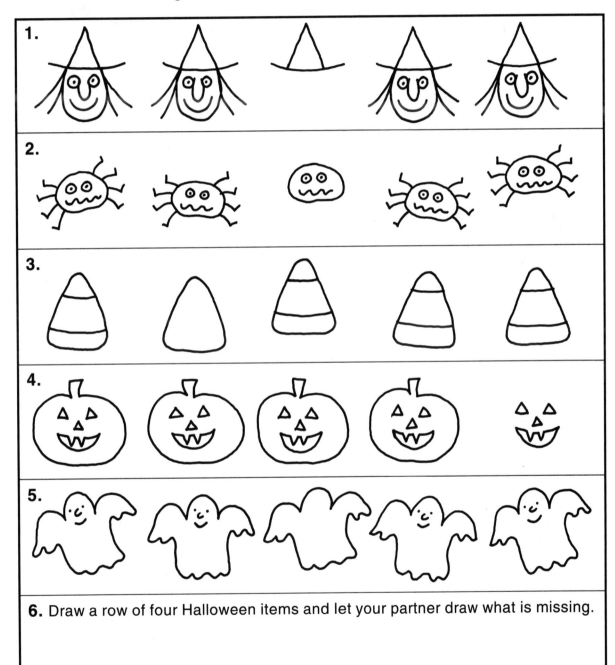

1.

2.

3.

4.

5.

6. Draw a row of four Halloween items and let your partner draw what is missing.

A NEW BREAKFAST CEREAL

DIRECTIONS: You have just created a new Halloween breakfast cereal! Now design the package it comes in. Then write an advertisement for it. Work with a partner to prepare a TV commercial for your cereal, and present it to the class.

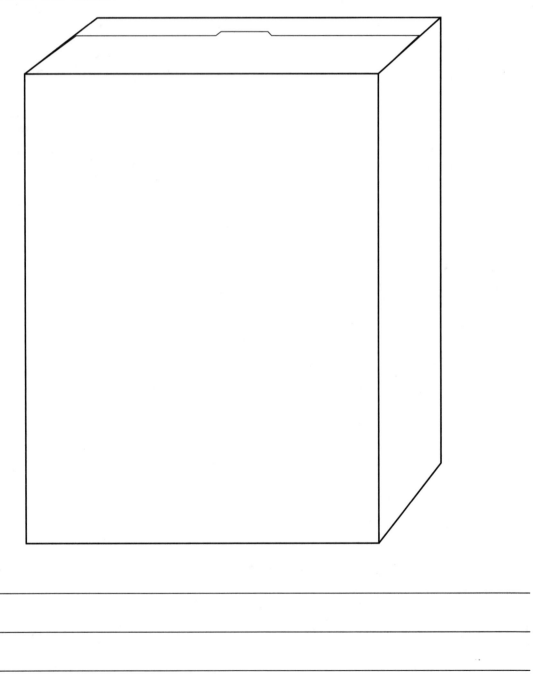

_____

_____

_____

_____

HALLOWEEN RESEARCH SKILLS

HAUNTED HISTORY

DIRECTIONS:

Work in small groups to find the answers to these questions and share your information with the class.

1. Where did Halloween come from?

2. Why do we wear scary costumes at Halloween?

3. Why did children start collecting candy on Halloween?

4. How did pumpkins become important at Halloween?

5. Why is Halloween celebrated in October and not in February?

6. What are some different Halloween traditions in other countries?

Learn more about the origin and traditions of Halloween using the following:

Halloween by Cass R. Sandak
(Crestwood House, 1990)

Halloween—A First Book by D. J. Herda
(Franklin Watts, 1983)

Halloween: Facts and Fun by Jill Hierstein-Morris
(Creatively Yours Publications, 1988)

Halloween: Holidays & Festivals by Robin May
(Rourke Enterprises, Inc., 1989)

SPOOKY SPOTS

DIRECTIONS: The monsters are getting ready to go trick-or-treating. Help them reach each spooky spot on the map on page 67 by filling in the blanks below. Use the compass rose.

1. Where is Mummy's Tomb? _____*west*_____ of Screaming Ghosts

2. Where is Sea Monster Lake? _____ of Dr. Frankenstein's Laboratory

3. Where are Screaming Ghosts? _____ of Tommy Troll

4. Where is the Haunted House? _____ of Mummy's Tomb

5. Where is Tommy Troll? _____ of Dr. Frankenstein's Laboratory

6. Where is Dr. Frankenstein's Laboratory? _____ of Screaming Ghosts

7. Where is Mummy's Tomb? _____ of the Haunted House

1. From Sea Monster Lake, go west to ___*Tommy Troll*___.

2. Go west from the Haunted House to _____.

3. Go south from Mummy's Tomb to _____.

4. From Dr. Frankenstein's Laboratory, go east to _____.

5. Go northeast from Tommy Troll to _____.

6. From the Haunted House, go northwest to _____.

7. Go south from the Haunted House to _____.

Name _____

SPOOKY SPOTS

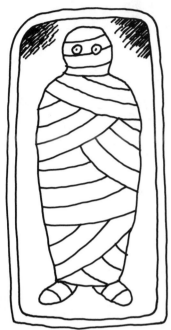

The Mummy's Tomb

The
Screaming
Ghosts

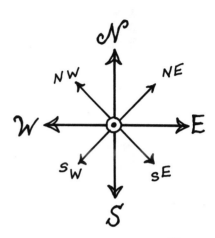

The Compass Rose

Dr. Frankenstein's
Laboratory

The Haunted House

Tommy Troll

Sea Monster Lake

HALLOWEEN COOKING

RECIPES

NUTTY PUMPKIN BREAD

Ingredients:

1 cup brown sugar	2 tsp. baking powder
1/3 cup shortening	1/2 tsp. salt
2 eggs	1/2 tsp. ground ginger
1 cup canned pumpkin	1/4 tsp. baking soda
1/4 cup milk	1/4 tsp. ground cloves
2 cups all-purpose flour	1/2 cup chopped walnuts

Directions:
1. Beat together brown sugar and shortening.
2. Add the eggs. Mix.
3. Add the canned pumpkin and milk. Mix.
4. Add the flour, baking powder, salt, ginger, baking soda, and cloves. Mix.
5. Add the walnuts. Mix.
6. Put the batter into a greased 9x5x3 loaf pan.
7. Bake at 350° for 55-60 minutes. Cool and slice.

HOMEMADE APPLESAUCE

Ingredients:

4 lbs. cooking apples	1 cinnamon stick (6 inches)
1 1/2 cups water	3/4 cup sugar

Directions:
1. Peel, core, and cut apples into quarter slices.
2. Place apples, water, and cinnamon stick in a 4-quart heavy pot.
3. Bring to boil. Reduce heat and simmer 10-15 minutes until apples are tender.
4. Remove cinnamon stick.
5. Mash apples with potato masher until smooth.
6. Add sugar, 1/4 cup at a time. Stir and taste for sweetness after each addition.
7. Applesauce is ready to serve, or cover and refrigerate.

GHOST POPS

MATERIALS:

lollipops
white tissue paper
twine or ribbon
black felt-tip marker

DIRECTIONS:

1. For each ghost, cut a 9-inch square of white tissue paper and a 9-inch piece of ribbon.

2. Center the lollipop on the tissue paper and tie a bow around it with the ribbon.

3. Draw a face on the "ghost" with the black felt-tip marker.

4. Have plenty of ghost pops on hand for your class Halloween party!

HALLOWEEN QUICK TRICKS AND NEAT TREATS

HAPPY JACK BULLETIN BOARD

Set the tone of your classroom with a student bulletin board.

DIRECTIONS:

1. Make a large, simple jack-o'-lantern out of orange butcher paper. Add facial features with a black marker.
2. Staple the jack-o'-lantern to a bulletin board at a height that is accessible to students.
3. Allow students to write *positive* messages about one another on the jack-o'-lantern. Discuss the messages. Younger students can dictate their messages to an adult to transcribe.

STUDENT AWARDS

Reinforce your students' efforts with these seasonal certificates!

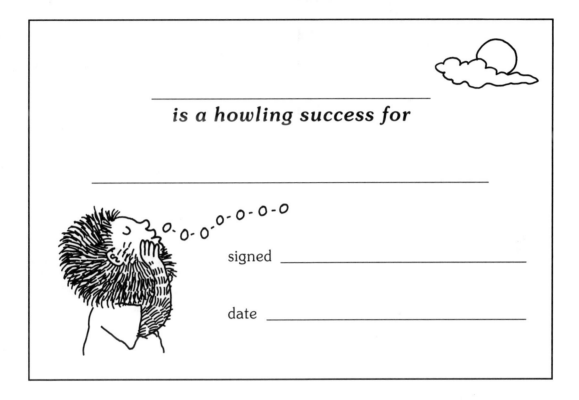

_____

is a howling success for

_____

signed _____

date _____

_____

shows a lot of team spirit!
Keep up the good work!

_____

signed _____

date _____

TEAM SPIRIT!

Name _____

BOOK REPORT CARD

Read a Halloween book, then grade it by filling out the following report card. Share your reactions with your classmates.

Name of reader: _____

Book title: _____

Author: _____

Illustrator: _____

Copyright date: _____

How would you rate the Halloween book you just read?

BOOK RATING SCALE

	☹ Yuk!	Not Very Good	☺ O.K.	Pretty Good	☺ Great!
Interesting characters					
Enjoyable story					
Good description					
Satisfying ending					
How would you rate this book overall?					

Comments: _____

_____

72

MIND YOUR MONSTERLY MANNERS

With a partner or a small group, have students write and illustrate an etiquette manual for monsters. Monsters need manners!

DEAR CASPER...

Students write an advice column for unhappy ghosts. What kinds of problems would a ghost have? How could they be solved?

With a partner, students role-play an unhappy ghost and the column writer.

As an extension, teach letter-writing format, how to address letters, etc.

GHOST WRITING

Using a cotton swab dipped in lemon juice, students write messages on white paper. Let dry, then have students hold the paper up to the light bulb. The ghostly message will magically turn brown.

HALLOWEEN READ-ALOUD

Read Halloween stories in the dark by the light of a flashlight. Play a tape of scary sounds in the background to add extra spookiness.

Ask parents, administrators, other teachers, students, or friends to read Halloween tales to the class.

GHOSTLY VOWEL HOWLS

Have students practice saying vowels using a veery scaary voice.

$\overline{aaa}$ $\overline{eee}$ $\overline{iii}$ $\overline{ooo}$ $\overline{uuu}$

HAUNTING PATTERN BOOKS

As a class, write Halloween versions of well-known pattern books. For example, *Brown Bear, Brown Bear, What Do You See?* by Bill Martin Jr. might become:

Black cat, Black cat, what do you see?
I see an orange pumpkin looking at me.

Orange pumpkin, orange pumpkin, what do you see?
I see a purple witch looking at me.

Purple witch, purple witch, what do you see?
I see a green goblin looking at me.

(and so forth)

CREATURE THEATER

Play one of the Halloween videos listed on page 79. Then let small groups retell the story as a play, short story, series of poems, or captioned illustrations.

MONSTER GEOGRAPHY

Ask small groups to find the geographical origins of legendary and movie monsters on a world map. For example: Dracula (Transylvania), Mummy (Egypt), Big Foot (Pacific Northwest), Loch Ness Monster (Scotland), Abominable Snowman (Nepal).

PLANT A PUMPKIN

Plant pumpkin seeds as a class project. Students measure and record their growth on a simple chart. Vary sunlight, water, and soil conditions for comparison.

SKELETAL SLEUTH

With the class, learn about the human skeletal system.

HALLOWEEN RESOURCES

LITERATURE

You may want to read through this list of Halloween favorites for a book that you can use for developing learning experiences in your classroom.

Because libraries catalogue children's picture books by the author's last name, this Halloween reference list has been organized in the same manner. You can systematically browse through your library picture book section with the reference list in hand.

Also be aware that many libraries place a special symbol on the spine of holiday books, which makes them even easier to find.

Many of the Halloween books listed here were found in a very helpful resource:

A to Zoo—Subject Access Guide to Children's Picture Books
Third Edition
Carolyn W. Lima & John A. Lima
R. R. Bowker, 1989.

This is an excellent guide to children's literature that organizes books by *subject theme* (i.e., Halloween) as well as by author. You can find many, many more Halloween-related children's books in this resource under such headings as: giants, ghosts, monsters, witches, and so forth.

A

Adams, Adrienne
A Halloween Happening, Macmillan Child Group, 1991.
A Woggle of Witches, Macmillan Child Group, 1985.

Adler, David A.
The Twisted Witch & Other Spooky Riddles, Bantam, 1986.

Alexander, Sue
Who Goes Out on Halloween?, Bantam, 1990.

B

Barth, Edna
Jack-o'-lantern, Houghton Mifflin, 1979.

**Berenstain, Stan &
Berenstain, Janice**
The Berenstain Bears Trick or Treat (with cassette), Random Books Young Read, 1991.

Bond, Felicia
The Halloween Performance, Harper-Collins Children's Books, 1987.

Bridwell, Norman
Clifford's Halloween, Scholastic, 1989.

Brown, Marc
Arthur's Halloween, Little, Brown and Co., 1983.

Bunting, Eve
Scary, Scary Halloween, Houghton Mifflin, 1988.

C

Calhoun, Mary
The Witch of Hissing Hill, Morrow Jr. Books, 1964.
Wobble the Witch Cat, Morrow Jr. Books, 1958.

Carlson, Nancy
Harriet's Halloween Candy (with cassette), Live Oak Media, 1985.

Carlson, Natalie Savage
Spooky and the Ghost Cat, Lothrop, 1985.
Spooky and the Wizard's Bats, Lothrop, 1986.
Spooky Night, Lothrop, 1982.

Carrick, Carol
Old Mother Witch, Houghton Mifflin, 1989.

Cassedy, Sylvia
The Best Cat Suit of All, Dial Books for Young Readers, 1991.

Charles, Donald
Shaggy Dog's Halloween, Children's, 1984.

Christelow, Eileen
Jerome and the Witchcraft Kids, Houghton Mifflin, 1990.

Cohen, Miriam
The Real-Skin Rubber Monster Mask, Greenwillow, 1990.

Coombs, Patricia
Dorrie and the Halloween Plot, Lothrop, 1976.

Corey, Dorothy
Will It Ever Be My Birthday?, A. Whitman, 1986.

Corwin, Judith Hoffman
Halloween Fun, Simon & Schuster Trade, 1983.

Crose, Mark
Halloween, Macmillan Child Group, 1991.

Cusick, Richie T.
Trick or Treat, Scholastic, 1989.

Cuyler, Margery
Sir William and the Pumpkin Monster, Henry Holt & Co., 1989.

D

De Paola, Tomie
My First Halloween, Putnam, 1991.

Degen, Bruce
Aunt Possum and the Pumpkin Man, HarperCollins Children's Books, 1977.

De Lage, Ida
The Old Witch and Her Magic Basket, Chelsea House, 1991.

Devlin, Wende & Harry Devlin
Cranberry Halloween, Macmillan Child Group, 1990.

Donnelly, Liza
Dinosaur's Halloween, Scholastic, 1988.

E

Embry, Margaret
The Blue Nosed Witch, Bantam, 1984.

F

Feczko, Kathy
Halloween Party, Troll, 1985.

Freeman, Don
Space Witch, Puffin Books, 1979.
Tilly Witch, Puffin Books, 1978.

G

Gantos, Jack
Rotten Ralph's Trick or Treat, Houghton Mifflin, 1988.

Gibbons, Gail
Halloween (with cassette), Live Oak Media, 1985.

Glovach, Linda
The Little Witch's Black Magic Book of Disguises, Prentice Hall, 1977.

Greene, Carol
The Thirteen Days of Halloween, Children's, 1983.

Guthrie, Donna
The Witch Who Lives Down the Hall, Harcourt Brace Javanovich, 1991.

H

Hautzig, Deborah
Little Witch's Big Night, Random Books for Young Readers, 1984.

Herman, Emily
Hubknuckles, Crown Books Young Read, 1985.

Hoban, Lillian
Arthur's Halloween Costume, HarperCollins Children's Books, 1986.

Howe, James
Scared Silly: A Halloween Treat, Morrow Jr. Books, 1989.

I

Irving, Washington
The Legend of Sleepy Hollow, Ideals, 1991.

J

Jasner, W. K.
Which Is the Witch?, Pantheon, 1979.

Johnston, Tony
Soup Bone, Harcourt Brace Javanovich, 1992.
The Vanishing Pumpkin, Putnam, 1990.

K

Keats, Ezra Jack
The Trip, Morrow, 1987.

Kellogg, Steven
The Mystery of the Flying Orange Pumpkin, Dial Books for Young Readers, 1983.

Kraus, Robert
How Spider Saved Halloween, Scholastic, 1988.

Kroll, Steven
The Biggest Pumpkin Ever, Scholastic, 1985.

Kunhardt, Edith
Trick or Treat, Danny!, Greenwillow, 1988.

L

Leedy, Loreen
The Dragon Halloween Party, Holiday House, 1986.

Low, Alice
The Witch Who Was Afraid of Witches, HarperCollins Children's Books, 1990.
Witch's Holiday, Pantheon, 1971.

M

Maestro, Giulio
Halloween Howls: Riddles That Are a Scream, Puffin Books, 1992.

Mariana
Miss Flora McFlimsey's Halloween, Lothrop, 1987.

Marshall, Edward
Space Case, Dial Books for Young Readers, 1982.

Martin, Bill
The Magic Pumpkin, Henry Holt & Co., 1989.

Meddaugh, Susan
The Witches' Supermarket, Houghton Mifflin, 1991.

Merriam, Eve
Halloween ABC, Macmillan Child Group, 1987.

Miller, Edna
Mouskin's Golden House, Simon & Schuster Trade, 1990.

Mooser, Stephen
The Ghost with the Halloween Hiccups, Avon, 1978.

Mueller, Virginia
A Halloween Mask for Monster, Puffin Books, 1988.

N

Nerlove, Miriam
Halloween, A. Whitman, 1992.

Nicoll, Helen
Meg and Mog, Puffin Books, 1976.

P

Peters, Sharon
Trick or Treat Halloween, Troll, 1980.

Prager, Annabelle
The Spooky Halloween Party (with cassette), Random Books for Young Readers, 1992.

Prelutsky, Jack
It's Halloween (with cassette), Scholastic, 1987.

Q

Quackenbush, Robert
Detective Mole and the Halloween Mystery, Simon & Schuster Trade, 1989.

R

Rockwell, Anne
Apples and Pumpkins, Macmillan Child Group, 1989.

Rylant, Cynthia
Henry and Mudge Under the Yellow Moon, Macmillan Child Group, 1992.

S

Schertle, Alice
Hob Goblin and the Skeleton, Lothrop, 1982.

Schweninger, Ann
Halloween Surprises, Puffin Books, 1986.

Sendak, Maurice
Where the Wild Things Are (with mini-Max doll), HarperCollins Children's Books, 1992.

Shecter, Ben
The Big Stew, HarperCollins Children's Books, 1991.

Stevenson, James
That Terrible Halloween Night, Morrow, 1990.

Stock, Catherine
Halloween Monster, Macmillan Child Group, 1990.

T

Titherington, Jeanne
Pumpkin, Pumpkin, Morrow, 1990.

U

Van Allsburg, Chris
The Mysteries of Harris Burdick, Houghton Mifflin, 1984.

W

Wiseman, Bernard
Halloween with Morris and Boris, Scholastic, 1986.

Z

Zolotow, Charlotte
A Tiger Called Thomas, Lothrop, 1988.

POETRY

Halloween Poems, selected by Myra Cohn Livingston, (Holiday House, 1989)

Halloween—Stories and Poems, edited by Caroline Feller Baur, (J. B. Lippincott, 1989)

It's Halloween, by Jack Prelutsky, (Scholastic, 1977)

Monster Poems, edited by Daisy Wallace, (Holiday House, 1976)

The Random House Book of Poetry for Children, selected by Jack Prelutsky, (Random House, 1982)

JOKES AND RIDDLES

Haunted House Jokes by Louis Phillips, (Puffin, 1988)

Hide-and-Go-Shriek Monster Riddles by Mercer Seltzer, (A. Whitman, 1990)

101 Monster Jokes by Sam Schultz, (Lerner Publications Co., 1982)

Riddles That Rhyme for Halloween Time by Leonard P. Kessler, (Gerrard, 1978)

Spooky Riddles by Marc Brown, (Beginner Books, 1983)

Spooky Riddles and Jokes by Joseph Rosenblum, (Sterling Publications Co., 1987)

The Twisted Witch and Other Spooky Riddles by David A. Adler, (Holiday House, 1985)

MUSIC

The Funny Songbook by Esther L. Nelson, (Sterling Publication Co., Inc., 1986)

Haunts and Taunts by Jean Chapman, (Children's Press International, 1983)

Marvin's Favorite Halloween Songs by Tom Armstrong, (Centerstream Publishing, 1985)

The New Novelty Songbook, (Hal Leonard Publications, 1989)

The Thirteen Days of Halloween by Carol Greene, (Regensteiner Publishing Enterprises, Inc., 1983)

RECORDED MUSIC

Halloween Fun (audio cassette), (Kimbo, 1989)

Halloween Hits (compact disc), (Rhino, 1991)

VIDEOS

Black Beard's Ghost (160 minutes) Walt Disney (not rated)

Disney's Halloween Treat (47 minutes), Walt Disney, Rated G

Disney's Mini Classic: Legend of Sleepy Hollow (33 minutes), Walt Disney, Rated G

Halloween Haunts (22 minutes), Walt Disney, Rated G

Halloween Is Grinch Night (30 minutes), Dr. Seuss, Rated G

Legend of Sleepy Hollow (98 minutes), Magnum Entertainment, Rated G

Scary Tales (43 minutes), Walt Disney, Rated G